Text: *Mark Richards*
Series editor: *Tony Bowerman*
Photographs: *Mark Richards, Steve Thompson/ www.sunstormphotography.com, Jean and Martin Norgate/ www.geog.port.ac.uk, Dalesman magazine, Shutterstock, Dreamstime, Carl Rogers*
Design: *Carl Rogers*

© *Northern Eye Books Limited 2015*

Mark Richards has asserted his rights under the Copyright, Designs and Patents Act, 1988 to be identified as the author of this work. All rights reserved.

This book contains mapping data licensed from the Ordnance Survey with the permission of the Controller of Her Majesty's Stationery Office. © Crown copyright 2015. All rights reserved. Licence number 100022856

Mapping sourced from Ordnance Survey

Northern Eye Books

ISBN 978-1-908632-34-0

A CIP catalogue record for this book is available from the British Library.

Cover: *The Howgills (Walk 6), by Steve Thompson*

First published in 2015 by
Northern Eye Books Limited
Northern Eye Books, Tattenhall, Cheshire CH3 9PX
Email: tony@northerneyebooks.com

For sales enquiries, please call 01928 723 744

'Linescape' artwork by Mark Richards
Inside cover: *Ingleborough from Kingsdale*
Title page: *Long Gill Beacon on Gt Shunner Fell*

Follow Mark on Twitter: *@fellranger1*

 Twitter: @Northerneyeboo
@Top10walks

Contents

Pennine perfection

Designated in 1954, the **Yorkshire Dales** cover 1,762 square kilometres/680 square miles of the central Pennines. As well as some of Yorkshire's most magnificent landscapes, the National Park also includes a corner of Cumbria, where the secluded Howgill Fells loom over the River Lune. 'Dales' is something of a misnomer, for in addition to the beautiful dales the area incorporates great tracts of wild moorland, the famous 'Three Peaks' and an intriguing industrial heritage.

Over 1,300 miles of rights of way allow walkers to explore all facets of the Park. In addition, almost 110,000 hectares of open access land has opened up endless possibilities for exploring this heady mix of limestone and gritstone scenery. Upwards of 8 million visitors a year enjoy this striking countryside with its picturesque stone villages.

The setting sun lights up the moors below Pen-y-ghent

The Yorkshire Dales' best fell walks

The term 'fell' derives from the Norse settlers and was applied here to areas of upland pasture. While the Lake District is defined by its soaring ridges, the Dales, as their name implies, are an intricate pattern of valleys set in a muted moorland landscape. Yet great hills exist — to enthral and enthuse even the most ardent hillgoer.

There is no better way of grasping the scale, beauty and extent of the Yorkshire Dales than from this fabulous compact of high fell tops. Each rooted in a dale, each dignified with unique prospects, all meriting walking as a richly rewarding company of hills.

"West Yorkshire is quite dramatic and beautiful, the crags and things."

David Hockney, contemporary artist

TOP 10 **Walks:** Fell Walks

THE FELLS OF THE YORKSHIRE DALES offer walkers both great character and moorland peace, with bubbling curlew and rising skylark sustaining that age-old connection of moorland pasture with verdant dale. There is range to the views and longevity in the scenes; prepare to step back in time as you climb the heights. Tackle and reflect on ten great little hills, including the enigmatic Three Peaks: Ingleborough, Pen-y-ghent and Whernside.

Great Whernside page 8

Buckden Pike page 14

Great Shunner Fell page 20

Wild Boar Fell page 26

Wharfedale's characteristic drystone walls and stone barns, or 'laithes'

Great Whernside

Wharfedale at its impressive best. A scenic walk that culminates on the paternal brow high above Kettlewell

What to expect:
Fell tracks, some damp ground

Distance/time: 12km/ 7½ miles. Allow 4 hours

Start: National Park car park in Kettlewell

Grid ref: SD 967 723

Ordnance Survey Map: Explorer OL30 Yorkshire Dales: *Northern & Central areas: Wensleydale & Swaledale*

After the walk: Kettlewell has two tearooms: Zarina's and The Cottage, and a brace of pubs: The Racehorses and The Blue Bell

Walk outline

A drove lane from Kettlewell gives a stirring start to proceedings, offering generous perspectives down Wharfedale and across the broad sweep of Great Whernside. It swings round by Tor Dyke to cross the road-pass to Coverdale and then climbs the high, tantalising brow of Great Whernside. From the rock-tor top, the route tumbles helter-skelter back down to the village.

Great Whernside

New visitors to Kettlewell are little aware of Great Whernside: it contrives to hang back as a deft presence, part of a consistent skyline, somewhat aloof, affording eastern shelter to the valley. Its single most worthy virtue is as a viewpoint, a summit from where one stands and stares: to gaze across succeeding Dales' ridges in a dreamlike state. With two fells in the National Park given the name Whernside — as sources of quern, or mill stones — it is rather curious that the lower and lesser-known of the pair has gained the grander title. This walk brings out its modest greatness.

Kettlewell barn

Golden plover

The Walk

1. Cross the road bridge and, from the **Blue Bell**, follow **Middle Lane** upstream, passing **Zarina's tearoom**. This becomes a minor road leading into the upper part of the village to where a signpost to 'Leyburn 1 in 4' ushers you sharp left with **Cam Gill Road**.

2. At the next bend, step off the tarmac, now heading up the stony **drove lane**.

As height is gained, stop and look back over the village and down the dale, showing off its U-shaped glacial profile.

From the first gate, the track becomes ever more a green-way.

Top Mere Lane *is an old sheep drove which was used to access* **Cam Pasture** *and the 'mere' pastures on the southern end of the Buckden Pike ridge.*

After the second gate, the drove lane is lost, but the open trackway continues to another gate, leading onto **Cam Head**. It later swings right to converge with the **Starbotton Cam Road** (bridle track) at a three-way fingerpost.

3. Keep right, signed 'Hunters Sleets'. After a gate, the path quickly loses the right-hand wall as it comes up into the trench of **Tor Dyke**. Though eroded by water in places there is strong evidence of the earthwork on top of a striking limestone scarp. The wall is rejoined and, after a sink hollow, in summer watch for a rash of nettles marching to a hand-gate and wall-stile. After this, the path drifts away from the wall some 20 metres, but be sure

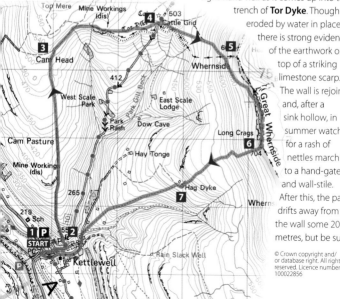

On top of the world: *The summit cairn and Ordnance Survey 'trig' point on Blackfell Top*

to keep right at a path fork, aiming to meet the road close to the cattle-grid.

4. Go straight across the road, signed 'Great Whernside', soon encountering further evidence of **Tor Dyke**. Go over the gated wall-stile and embark on an unfortunate passage of unavoidably marshy moor as best you can. 'Dry' land resumes as the slope steepens. The route slips through an eroded gully and slants right to cross a stile where a rising fence meets a wall.

5. The popular path holds to the western slope, gradually gaining height on **Blackfell Top**. *The summit is occupied by a large cairn and a concrete OS pillar at 704 metres/2,310 feet.*

There is scope here to explore the gritstone outcropping and boulders in all their fanciful, weathered forms. There is even a shelter set, it seems, upon a tumulus.

The name Whernside confirms the coarse gritstone liberally available on the plateau. The edge was once a source of querns, or watermill grindstones.

Rolled gold: *Looking down across the rolling fells not far below the summit*

You may also hear the mournful cry of golden plovers, which nest on the plateau.

6. When eventually you wrench yourself from this heavenly height, head south, rounding the rocks to find the descending path. Recent step-pitching lower down the steep bank makes the descent easier than in former times. At the lap of the slope though, damp, peaty moorland has to be negotiated. Tread carefully to minimise your impact where you can. As elsewhere on the fell, **yellow-topped posts** act as a guide.

7. Eventually, a **conical cairn** marks the lip of a broken edge. The downward path is littered with loose stones en route to **Hag Dyke**.

8. Pass round the long building, a **Scouts' activity centre**, via gates and then walk along the access track to the exit gate. Veer half-left from the track, guided by the footpath fingerpost down the pasture. Go through a wall gap, slanting part-left by a tall fingerpost to a hand-gate just above the **Dowber Gill valley**.

The continuing path leads through a double-gated wall-stile succeeded by a hand gate after which the ridge opens

out. Passing a second fingerpost, bear right at a fork as the path comes off the ridge pasture via a stile. A gate leads onto a green track, which drops, via another stile, to a gate and gated wall-stile. Bear tight right beside **Dowber Gill Beck** to come onto a track and cross the bridge. Follow the lane through **Town Head** and back to the car park to complete the walk. ♦

Tor Dyke

Historians think this earthwork was thrown up to mark the boundary of the kingdom of Craven, a post-Roman territory northwest of Elmet, reaching to the rivers Ribble, Wharfe and Aire. The dyke once formed a line between Anglian invaders and native Britons. Some 2,000 metres long, this manmade ditch and bank feature marshalled access from upper Wharfedale into lower Wensleydale via Coverdale — presumably a significant pass at the time.

The conical summit cairn on Buckden Pike

Buckden Pike

Encounter an old lead mine and enjoy a bracing ridge-top with spacious views

What to expect:
Hill tracks and paths; some spongy moor

Distance/time: 8km/ 5 miles. Allow 3½ hours

Start/finish: National Park pay and display car park off Buckden Wood Lane at the northern end of Buckden in upper Wharfedale

Grid ref: SD 943 773

Ordnance Survey Map: Explorer OL30 Yorkshire Dales: *Northern & Central areas: Wensleydale & Swaledale*

After the walk: The Buck Inn, Village Café and West Winds Tearoom, all in Buckden

Walk outline

This perfect round walk revels in long moorland horizons with a great sense of space. The route climbs south on a good turf trail before switching north to reach the long-abandoned lead mine at the head of Buckden Beck. Complete the ascent to the summit ridge of Buckden Pike with its memorial cross and crowning cairn. The descent is on a new trail that leads down to Buckden Rake and the final sylvan flourish of Rakes Wood.

Buckden Pike

This is the fourth highest fell in the National Park and commands a fabulous all-round view, notably to the west where Fountains Fell, Pen-y-ghent (walk 10) and Ingleborough (walk 9) tantalise. There is a genuine sense of remote elevation; a great fell landscape with far horizons — a proper reward for the day's endeavour. Strong walkers will happily combine Buckden Pike with Great Whernside in a 15-mile trek from Kettlewell, backtracking south from Tor Mere Top on Starbotton Out Moor either via Top Mere Road or Walden Road, Starbotton and the Dales Way.

Buckden Gavel lead mine

Wild thyme

The Walk

1. From the **village car park**, step on to the track leading to the gate with National Trust and wooden path signs. Ignore the open track ahead, signposted 'Cray High Bridge'. Instead, turn sharp right up by the wall, signposted 'Path leading to Buckden lead mine'. Rise to go through a gate and pass the water treatment works, then bear right by the wall to a sheep-pen.

2. Ford **Buckden Beck** on a track that gives lovely views of the cascading stream. The path hairpins and continues through gates, passing beneath a thorn scrub bank and above a wood. As the woodland ends, so the track embarks on a steep ascent with a wall on the left. *This path gives handsome views of Wharfedale, good reason to stop, take a breather and soak up the setting. Contrast the sharp division between the green wooded strath and the sweeping tiered uplands.* The path heads uphill through old gateways and switches sharp left at a 'path' fingerpost.

3. Soon with a broken wall on the left, rise to a fingerpost where a path from Starbotton

merges from the right. The turf path winds on uphill via old wall gateways until it passes through a gate leading to a wooden stile at a wall corner. The path now skips by **sink hollows** and leaves the immediate company of the wall as it traverses the rough fell-side to come into the dale-head of **Buckden Beck**.

Here, walkers can inspect the vestiges of the **Buckden Gavel lead mine**, *opened in 1697 and worked until 1877 when the expansion of lead mining in Spain undercut the price of domestic metal.*

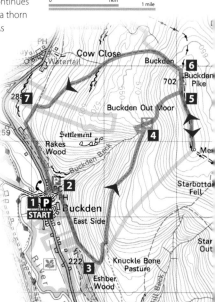

War memorial: *The Polish Memorial Cross marks the site of a WWII bomber crash*

Many a Yorkshire miner left the area at this time to further their skills in Spain or Pittsburgh in Pennsylvania.

The mine entrance arch is most striking. That it is so low will pose questions about working conditions. During their working week, the miners lived in a stone hut, known as a 'shop', close to the mine entrance. The remnants of work sheds, a long, spoil extraction tip and characteristic bare, lead-poisoned spoil are fascinating to inspect.

4. The path goes left by the wall and then up the bank, drifting right to climb the steep bank directly above the **adit** — an opening into the mine. A clear fell path then leads on to the ridge, latterly following an ascending wall to reach a ladder-stile.

5. Before you cross you might like to wander south beside the ridge wall to cross a ladder-stile and inspect the **Polish Memorial Cross**, *a poignant reminder of a wartime air crash, with its quirky fox head.* Backtrack and cross the aforementioned ladder-stile to visit

Below the scarp: *A moorland path descends the western slopes of Buckden Pike*

the **summit of Buckden Pike** (702 metres/2,303 feet).

6. The path draws naturally off the summit in a north-westerly direction. Recent path restoration work is evident, including slab steps. Lower down, a gravel trail snakes on until a turf path is rejoined. This leads through a wall hand-gate. After the next gateway, a limestone scar adds close interest as you look down on the hamlet of Cray.

The sheep-cropped pasture, overlaying the limestone bedrock, is dotted with sink holes. These are places where surface water drains away, swallowed into cracks in the limestone bedrock to pursue a secret underground journey before reappearing in minor gill resurgences.

Further gateways and a gate lead down to **Buckden Rake**.

Buckden Rake was originally a Roman road linking forts at Ilkley (Olicana) with Bainbridge (Virosidum) in Wensleydale. The presence of these forts strongly implies active Roman lead mining in the Dales.

7. Go through the metal gate at the three-way sign, aiming for 'Buckden'.

Notice the curved wall bield over the wall down to the right.

The green track becomes a stony way, leading on by a gate down through **Rakes Wood**, *all the time enjoying lovely intimate views of the valley, its trees and pastures. In spring, primroses adorn the banks in the wood.* Lower down, steep scree spills towards the track, adding a further textural dimension to the experience. A gate leads on to pasture and the next gate puts you back where you began to complete the walk. ♦

Langstrothdale Chase

Langstrothdale Chase refers to the red deer hunting preserve established in upper Wharfedale in the 12th century under the Earls of Northumberland. It was administered by a 'Forest Keeper', living here until 1534. The laws were strict and impacted on local people, controlled through a 'Woodmote', or forest court, which met every 40 days. The name, Buckden, meaning 'the valley for the deer buck', is a reminder of its past.

Gritstone and grass on Great Shunner Fell

Great Shunner Fell

A steady ascent with the Pennine Way, impressive summit views and a secret valley

What to expect:
Fell and moorland paths with peaty tracks, stone paving over wetter sections

Distance/time: 17km/ 10½ miles. Allow 6 hours

Start: Verge parking at the western end of Hardraw

Grid ref: SD 866 913

Ordnance Survey Map: Explorer OL30 Yorkshire Dales: *Northern & Central areas: Wenselydale & Swaledale*

After the walk: The Green Dragon Inn, Hardraw. Otherwise, the nearby town of Hawes is abundantly served by tea-rooms and pubs

Walk outline

From Hardraw, the route rises with the Pennine Way to culminate on the moorland summit. It backtracks, then veering off the ridge to visit the shy hamlet of Cotterdale. A fell-foot path leads out of the valley to reconnect with the out-walk. Most walkers you'll meet are intent on the National Trail, making your mission feel subtly different and more engaged with the landscape.

Great Shunner Fell

For half a century, Pennine Way walkers have traipsed diligently over this remote hill-top, the third highest in the National Park, connecting Hardraw with Keld. Other visitors of the peak-bagging persuasion gather in Lovely Seat off the Buttertubs road for their day's trek.

Quite appropriately, the fell-name derives from the Viking 'sionar' meaning 'look-out'. At 716 metres/2,349 feet, there is no doubt that should you be lucky enough to arrive in half decent conditions you will be treated to a sumptuous and extensive panorama, with distant glimpses of Lakeland's giants, while to the north are the Howgills and the Cross Fell range, the highest ground in the Pennine chain.

Cotterdale barn and pines

Red squirrel

The Walk

1. Beyond the **old school-house** west of the road bridge, find a lane signposted **Pennine Way** 'FP Thwaite'. Follow this gated way up to the fell.

2. Hold to the open track, keeping left where it forks with the Pennine Way. As you ascend, take note of a footpath bearing left, signposted 'Cotterdale': this will be your return path after visiting the summit. Winding up by **old quarry works**, pass through a gate/ladder-stile on to the open fell proper at **Hearne Top** — with a walled fold close by on the left. You've now reached the edge of the **High Abbotside** moorland regeneration scheme.

3. Turn right off the turf trail with the Pennine Way 'FP Thwaite'. You are now very much on rough fell terrain as you come up by a **cairn** with a bield over to the left on **Humesett**. The first of several peaty stretches protected by **flagstone paving** is encountered as you pass to the left of **Black Hill Moss**. There is some wet ground to cross before the ridge steepens to reach a **large cairn** at **Bleak Haw**. Continue to a further **cairn** at **Crag End Beacon**. Thereafter, more paving leads duly to a second notable step in the ridge at **Hearne Head**.

There is a wonderful irony in all this stone paving, as it was invariably salvaged from old mill buildings. You might know of Ewan MacColl's song The

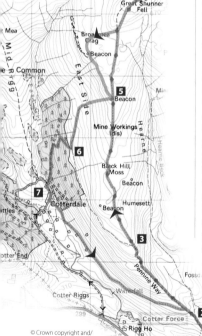

High-level paving: *Much of the upper section of the ridge is paved with stone slabs*

Manchester Rambler, *which relates to the cotton mill work-slaves finding their Sunday freedom on the Pennine moors.*

The path weaves its way across peaty ground to a fence-stile and then on to the **summit cross-wall** on **Great Shunner Fell**.

4. Backtracking, descend the first step in the ridge. At this point, you may veer right over pathless, damp moor to the prominent **Long Gill Beacon** perched on the edge overlooking Cotterdale. Then follow the quad track along the edge to **Crag End Beacon**. Otherwise, stick with the **Pennine Way** over familiar territory to reach the same spot.

5. From Crag End Beacon, break off the ridge to the right, heading down the steep slope with no hint of a path. Descend **East Side** to the fragmentary remains of the **Victorian colliery** where you'll find a track, now regularly used by gamekeepers' quad bikes. This heads south-southwest, passing large **sink hollows**. It then veers sharp right on

Welcome windbreak: *The stone cross shelter on the summit of Great Shunner Fell*

meeting a joining track emerging from **Cotterdale Woods** plantation at a gate.

6. Bear down into the conifers, quickly emerging from the dark into light where a great swathe of the plantation has been felled. The track zig-zags down, guided by bridleway signs. Watch for the signpost that ushers you right – off the open track and on to a confined path that skips over a plank to go through a hand-gate by picnic tables. The path switches right to cross a wooden bridge spanning **East Gill** and follows the track

into the **hamlet of Cotterdale** — *a precious haven for the native red squirrel.*

7. Thread through the short 'street' to cross the footbridge signposted 'Hardraw 3 miles'. From the hand-gate, traverse the meadow and go through a narrow wall gate. After a ditch with a plank across it, continue to a wall squeeze stile. At the next gated squeeze-stile, step over a slatted plank to reach a wall-gate above a fenced spring. The path contours to a squeeze-stile above a stone barn. After a wall gateway, it rises from the next field barn above the line of telegraph poles to cross a broken wall and fence-stile. The

next enclosure has young deciduous trees planted below spoil banks. A fence and then wall stiles are crossed as one moves out of **Cotterdale** proper and enters **Wensleydale**. Further gateways lead on above a large sheepfold. The path rises over a broken wall and then a wall squeeze stile, traversing the rough pasture to reconnect with the **Pennine Way**. Go right to re-enter the walled lane to complete the walk. ♦

Cotterdale

Cotterdale is an exquisite cul-de-sac side valley of the Ure. In the 19th century, there was a thriving mining community here; now only 12 cottages remain, and today grouse moor management, shepherding and forestry shape the local economy. The High Abbotside moorland regeneration scheme is the largest in the Pennines, and aims both to increase black grouse numbers and support a wider diversity of moorland flora and fauna.

White Kirk waterfall in Ais Gill

Wild Boar Fell

Wonderful walking from a limestone gorge via a scenic sub-scarp to reach two high summit plateaux

What to expect:
Mostly rough moorland paths, both sheep and man-made

Distance/time: 13km/ 8 miles. Allow 5 hours

Start/finish: Layby between Cotegill Bridge and the bridge over the Settle-Carlisle Railway

Grid ref: SD 774 970

Ordnance Survey Map: Explorer OL2 Yorkshire Dales: *Southern & Western areas: Whernside, Ingleborough & Pen-y-ghent*

After the walk: The Black Bull, Nateby or The Moorcock Inn, Garsdale Head

Walk outline

A great moorland walk with an early adventure in an almost impenetrable limestone gorge. It climbs in an exaggerated curve along a line of sinkholes to step up on to the rising scarp and reach the summit plateau. Adding Swarth Fell as a second summit 'bag' lends a fabulous backward perspective on Wild Boar Fell and rounds off a thoroughly good fell day.

Wild Boar Fell

We do not know how long it is since wild swine roamed these fell-sides, but the very fell-name remains a clarion call to climb. The valley name Mallerstang also resonates with the wild setting, bringing its own magic. It forms a deep trough beneath high edges where the River Eden is born — the only river in England to flow entirely north to its maritime freedom. The valley harbours castle ruins, none more enigmatic than Pendragon, named, probably for romantic effect, after the fifth-century father of the legendary King Arthur. We cannot fathom the veils and mists of myth and mystery, all clouding history — let's just hope your walk is blessed with more climatic clarity.

Wild Boar Fell cairn

Wild boar

The Walk

1. How comical is this? We walk downhill to start the climb as we follow the road north over the railway bridge.

This is **Aisgill Summit**, *the highest point on the Settle-Carlisle Railway at 356 metres/1,168 feet. The 25th anniversary of the saving of this famous line was celebrated in 2014. Happily, the service has thrived since it was threatened with closure in the 1980s.*

Coming down to **Aisgill Farm** and having crossed **Aisgill Beck**, watch for a footpath sign immediately after the well-tended cottage on the left.

2. From the gate, a green track leads up to pass under the **railway viaduct**. Continue in harmony with the **gorge**, with the railing fence close by on the left initially. Climb over the first **gorge brow** to approach the top of a **great waterfall cleft**. (This would have denied you access if you had stayed beside the beck.) You now have two choices. Either stay intimate with the **White Kirk gorge** to view the resurgence and the ultimately no-go upper gill cleft. If you do this, you will later have to backtrack to escape. Alternatively, bear immediately right up the bank, on to the moor. In all events that is where you next have to be as the walk heads north once more.

3. Evidence of a path is patchy: a shepherd's quad bike tracks suggest a route over damp rush ground to reach the

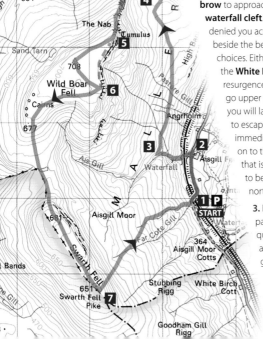

On the edge: *A cluster of conical stone cairns perched on the lip of High White Scar*

fell wall. Now there is a path, which is followed to the first of a sequence of fenced potholes and sinks on **Angerholme Pots**. *The sheer number of hollows will lend fascination to this stage of the walk, each subtly different from its neighbour.* Hold their line, though you should make a point of attaining the leading edge of the limestone sub-scarp, where a **cairn** is perched beside a **defunct TV aerial**. Follow this edge, coming by a broken wall and on

to a small area of clints by a hoary old **sheepfold**.

4 Join the **Pennine Bridleway**, marked by stakes, on its rise out of **Mallerstang** bound for **High Dolphinsty**. Coming up into the notch, ignore the acorn waymarked trail where it goes through a hand-gate — ultimately to descend to Stennerskeugh. Our mission is to stick with the rising ridge, climbing south-southwest with no complications on to **The Nab**. A fine moment to relish.

5. You may choose to follow the inviting edge to the wind-break wall, gazing

Moving drama: *Cloud shadows scurry across Mallerstang Edge*

down upon the gritstone scarp above **Yoadcomb** (*Viking for 'high valley of the old mare'*) and noting an impressive pinnacle arête. Most walkers though will opt to head directly to the **stone column** marking the **summit of Wild Boar Fell** at 708 metres/2,323 feet.

The view from west to north includes the Howgill Fells, High Street and Helvellyn ranges and the Eden backed by the high Pennines, centred on Cross Fell.

From the column, bear southeast over the pooled plateau to reach the wind-break wall and, crossing the fence, the cluster of **cairns on High White Scar**.

6. Follow the fence west-southwest, sweeping round above **The Band** of **Aisgill Head** to descend into the broad depression. The onward march of the ridge wall provides a sure guide on to the next top, where a small wind-break wall and then a chunky **cairn** will arrest your progress for a few minutes at the northern tip and **summit of Swarth Fell** (681 metres/2,234 feet). *It's a grand spot to consider the sturdy scarp of Wild Boar Fell.* The ridge path dances on south-eastward to the minor top of **Swarth Fell Pike**. The cairn is perched

on the other side of the fence, accessed by a stile. A second **cairn**, a little further down, marks the end of the ridge walk.

7. Now we break left from the ridge fence, with no semblance of a path, aiming northeast.

Descend **Aisgill Moor** by crossing **Far Cote Gill** and later following **Near Cote Gill** downhill. After a **disused quarry** at the confluence of the gills, reach a stile directly opposite your parked car to complete the walk. ♦

Towards a 'Greater Dales'?

Gritstone set upon a bed of limestone is a common feature of the Yorkshire Dales. Here it's given a new twist: you're walking entirely in Cumbria. Human political divisions don't always match physical relief — when high ridges become boundaries, for example. Better that natural unity wins the day. If proposals to extend the National Park further into Cumbria get the go ahead, more of this inspiring landscape will be protected.

Low evening light illuminates the corrugated flanks of the Howgills

Randygill Top

A free-flowing wander over open grassy terrain, that distinctive ingredient of the Howgill Fells

What to expect:
A mix of good tracks and fell paths

Distance/time: 13km/ 8 miles. Allow 5 hours

Start: Broad grassy verge where the re-aligned side road meets the A685.

Grid ref: NY 685 050

Ordnance Survey Map: Explorer OL19 *Howgill Fells & Upper Eden Valley*

After the walk: B's Tearoom at Bessy Beck Trout Fishery in Newbiggin-on-Lune

Walk outline

The walk first climbs onto the Hooksey ridge from where you should give yourself ample time to study the deep incursion of Bowderdale. Randygill Top is attained from the high saddle of Leathgill Bridge. Turning northeast to Green Bell, the source of the River Lune, the route then hurtles down unfettered into the hamlet of Weasdale — the 'valley of the weasel'. Apart from the pull up from Leathgill Bridge, the gradients are largely easy.

Randygill Top

The name Randygill Top is derived from the Viking personal-name 'Randulf'. It is a great place to study the Howgills — the slopes rising to The Calf (Walk 6) are a fine sight. In the distance, to the immediate left of Yarlside, is Whernside (Walk 8); left of that is Ingleborough (walk 9) and Great Knoutberry (Walk 7) beyond Dentdale. Westward, the Lakeland fells from Coniston Old Man to Carrock Fell draw the eye; closer in, arcing from east to south, are Wild Boar Fell (Walk 4) and Baugh Fell embracing the headstream of the Rawthey.

Green Bell summit

Weasel

The Walk

1. Follow the slip road west to a minor junction where an access bridge heads off to the right, under the main road. Turn left here via a cattle-grid to

pass **Brow Foot**, ignoring the inviting footpath that makes a curious start through the wicket-gate in the tall wall. Keep with the minor road, forking left at the top of the rise — now with the open road signposted to 'Scar Sikes'.

2. Where this swings left towards the farm, continue straight on, now following the **tractor track** heading south. It goes through a gate and, beyond that, a fence gap. As the adjacent wall on the right falters, the track splits. Choose the left-hand path. This ascends on to a low ridge with a bield wall on the first minor crest. The green way persists. Stick with it, heading on to the shoulder of **Hooksey** to come on to the ridge-top. Trend right for special views into the long trough of Bowderdale to the west; to the east are Green Bell and the head of Weasdale — most attractive! The highest point on the fell has a tiny **cairn** at 586 metres/1,923 feet.

3. The quad bike path rushes helter-skelter down into the saddle of **Leathgill Bridge**, a novel use of the term 'bridge'. The slope ahead is abrupt, but without incident and you are soon homing in on the small **summit cairn of Randygill Top** (624 metres/2,047 feet).

4. Now turn northeast with the ridge path over **Stockless** and **Spengill Head**. Heading up a groove, the footpath veers

Cairn and able?: *The step-aside summit cairn on Hunthoof Pike*

left, but all intentions will be towards the **summit OS column on Green Bell** (605 metres/1,988 feet).

The name of the fell attests to its distinctive shape and renowned grazing. There is certainly little hint of moorland species above and beyond the tough grass.

5. Energetic Red Rose Lancastrians will have this as a pilgrimage, specifically targeting the **spring source of Dale Beck** on the north-eastern flanks of the fell where their great river, the Lune, is born. *The river name is thought to derive from the old Irish slàn, meaning 'health-giving' — hence the city-name Lancaster — and there is little doubt that this brief detour will invigorate you.*

Other folk will be content to abide with the regular path which now sets course north, gaining lovely views into the side valley of Great Swindale. Off to the left you will spot a cairn on **Hunthoof Pike**. This rocky knoll-top viewpoint deserves a visit over pathless terrain. Swiftly regaining the popular trail, sweep on down the fell by the curiously named if featureless knoll **Stwarth**.

Ridgeway: *The shepherds' quad bike track along the top of Hooksey*

Old Norse vernacular names litter this landscape, with many, like this one, hard to decipher. This hill-name might be a local twist on swarthy, meaning 'dark' or 'in the shadows'. The Viking settlement in the area appears to have begun in the ninth century, hence the obvious mix and marriage of place-names. Most of these Viking settlers came from Ireland, sweeping into the area from the Clyde to the mouth of the Lune. In the 10th century all of this area was known as Cumbria, a Celtic word meaning 'the land of our fellow countrymen'.

6. Where a waymarker post indicates a fork in the way, keep left, heading downhill to join a track above **Will Gill**, which means 'wild valley'. This track runs above the enclosure wall, later drifting naturally down through the rush-beset pasture to the open road.

7. Turn left, passing a **ruined farmstead** to reach a junction, with **Weasdale Nursery** on the right. Here turn left by **Weasdale Farm**, with its proud 'Rough Fell Country' plaque. Go through the road-gate and over **Weasdale Beck**. Chuckling at the 'Keep out of the gutter' notice, climb to the recently renovated **Cow Bank** with its raucous rookery.

8. The road ends, but a bridle-track continues through a galvanised gate and across rather damp pasture to a wooden gate. This provides access to an **old drove lane** — again in marshy circumstances. Follow this lane. It later loses its flanking wall to reach a gate and the roadway from **Gars**, returning to the starting point to complete the walk. ♦

Rough Fell sheep

While walkers will delight in spotting small herds of wild fell ponies on the Howgills, they should be more than transfixed when encountering the indigenous sheep on these fells. Known either as Rough Fell or Kendal Rough, these animals have a rare and arresting beauty. Bred for their wool, which is coarse and ideal for making carpets, they were once the mainstay of the thriving, nineteenth-century Kendal carpet industry.

Green track heading towards White Fell

The Calf

Revel in sumptuous views over the Howgills as you follow green tracks from in-bye pastures on to open fell

What to expect:
Steep fell paths and grassy tracks

Distance/time: 13km/ 8 miles. Allow 5½ hours

Start/finish: Park on the beckside verge adjacent to Holy Trinity Church, in the hamlet of Howgill

Grid ref: SD 634 950

Ordnance Survey Map: Explorer OL19 *Howgill Fells & Upper Eden Valley*

After the walk: A range of cafés and pubs in Sedbergh

Walk outline

This walk to the ultimate ground of the exquisite Howgills follows sleek-lined slopes and curvaceous ridges above deeply grooved lonesome dales. To a large extent unfettered by fences, it is a wanderer's heaven. Here roam the curly-horned, bold white Rough Fell sheep, and the dusk brown fell ponies. In the skies is a wonderful abundance of bird-life. If I betray a passion for these hills, then, after this walk, I hope you will too.

The Calf

The Calf is the very essence of Howgill walking: neither Lakes nor Pennines, they are utterly unique. To confirm their distinction from the Dales, the Howgills' bedrock is allied to the core Cumbrian mountains, being divided from the Carboniferous rocks by the Dent fault. Casually and fleetingly observed by millions of travellers from the motorway and West Coast Mainline railway — and adored by all who wander willingly into their sanctuary — they form a compact triangle of high country bounded by the Lune on the west and north and Rawthey to the south.

Howgills' walkers

Fell pony

The Walk

1. From **Holy Trinity Church**, walk back to the road gate and bear left with **Howgill Lane**.

Before Holy Trinity, sitting beside Chapel Beck, was built in 1838, the cottage on the far bank was the parish church of the scattered community of Howgill. (The parish-name simply means 'hill stream'.)

Howgill Lane rests on the course of a Roman road, a day's march between forts at Low Borrow Bridge, Burrow and Lancaster.

*At the top of the rise, cross the ladder-stile before you reach the right-hand barn at **Gate Side**.*

2. Contour round by the concrete yard wall, to go through the gate in the field corner. Join the shelf path curving right to left. Go through the next gate and ford the gill. Rise to a ladder-stile and then slant up right to go through the wall gap above the barbed wire-wrapped signpost. Keep beside the wall to go through a metal field-gate and follow the track up to a gate. Enter the yard, passing the farmhouse at **Castley**.

3. Head uphill along the access track, quickly bearing right through a gate to follow a walled lane. This opens on to the fell at a gate beside a sheepfold.

Ahead, a grand circle of billowing fells, resembling a huddle of bald elders, embraces the headstreams of Chapel Beck.

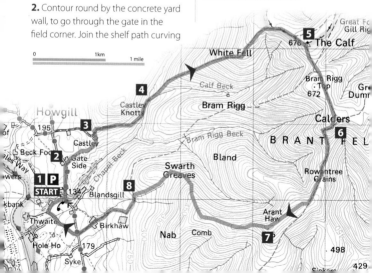

Sleek ridges: *Looking northwest from White Fell towards Fell Head and the Whinfell range*

Keep to the grass track, which gradually descends to ford the beck.

4. The work of the day begins with a steady climb on a consistent green trail up **White Fell**.

The fell-name reflects the pale grass found hereabouts.

The plateau is reached with a cheer, although the scenery throughout has given all the excuses in the world to take many a breather to glory in the sleek-

sloped ridges characteristic of these fells. The trail curves right and, where it forks, keep southeast, easing up to the OS column on the **summit of The Calf**.

5. Keep ahead on the engineered trail heading east-southeast. Descending through a depression, cross the course of a bridle-path. This trends southwest and then west down **Bram Rigg** and might be used as a fine way to shorten the round. But, for so little extra effort, it's worth sticking to the high ground, climbing over **Bram Rigg Top**, to reach the modest **cairn on Calders**. From

Like great beasts: *Smooth and sinuous shoulders on the Howgills just before sunset*

here, you get a new dimension south to the Yorkshire Three Peaks.

All of this section is blessed with fabulous views, not only of the Howgill ridges, but also east to Wild Boar Fell.

6. The ridge trail veers down by the netting fence and turns acutely left as it continues onto **Rowantree Grains**. Coming over the brow to find a **wooden guide board**, bear right, holding to the gentle rise of the ridge to reach the **summit of Arant Haw** and a slightly more substantial **cairn** than the one on Calders.

7. A steady path leads west, declining along the comparatively narrow ridge until a fork is encountered. Ignore the path bearing left which goes off via Nab towards Sedbergh. *It is on a popular run followed by staff and students of Sedbergh School, where fitness has always been a prime ingredient of education.*

Go right onto the final proper crest, marked by a **small cairn**. From here, a quad bike track acts as a sure guide north down to **Swang Head** — *swang meaning 'a swampy piece of ground'.* From here, drift left with a green track to join the bridle track from Bram Rigg as you ford **Eller Mire Beck**.

8. Go through the twin-gated fold in the intake wall. The track makes a right turn at the next gate and leads down, via gates and through the farmyard at **Birkhaw**, to meet **Howgill Lane**. Go straight over with **New Road** and, at the cattle-grid, bear right. Passing a cluster of cottages, including a former mill, you'll reach **Chapel Beck** and the **parish church** to complete the walk. ♦

Howgill Lane

Howgill Lane follows the course of a Roman road that linked forts at Kirkby Thore (Bravoniacum) and Lancaster (Calunium). It passes through what is often referred to as the Lune Gorge, the impressive passage through the hills that is threaded by the M6 motorway and West Coast Mainline. A little north of Howgill is Low Borrowbridge fort. Recent excavations have revealed its bath-house, important for a healthy military garrison.

Artengill Beck tumbles down Dent Fell

Great Knoutberry Hill

A moorland traverse sandwiched between quiet roads and old colliery tracks, with a possible scenic railway ride

What to expect:
Minor roads; tracks; spongy moorland paths

Distance/time: 12km/ 7½ miles. Allow 4½ hours

Start: Park in the short approach lane to Dent Station, OR where the bridleway leaves the Coal Road (SD 779 881)

Grid ref: SD 764 875

Ordnance Survey Map: Explorer OL2 Yorkshire Dales: *Southern & Western areas: Whernside, Ingleborough & Pen-y-ghent*

After the walk: The Sportsman's Inn in Cowgill; two tearooms and two pubs in Dent

Walk outline

From the highest mainline railway station in England, this walk climbs over Great Knoutberry Hill before delving into the enchanting green hollow of Dentdale. It follows the Coal Road up from Dent Station and uses the lateral colliery track to embark on an up-and-over traverse of Great Knoutberrry Hill before descending via Arten Gill and the hamlet of Cowgill to climb back up the Coal Road. The area's industrial past has since been subdued by time.

Dent Station

Great Knoutberry

The keen botanist will search in vain in the spartan moorland herbage on this walk for the orange-tinged fruits after which the fell is named. Like so many plants that might occur naturally in this setting, the cloudberry, or knoutberry as it is known locally, has been vanquished in recent centuries by a monoculture of sheep grazing.

To many visitors, the expansive plateau may seem uninviting and barren, but the hauntingly long views of Lakeland and Dales' horizons are pure magic.

Cloudberry

The Walk

1. Step back onto the **Coal Road** and turn right to follow it uphill, beside **Monkey Beck**, to where the 'Pennine Bridleway' is signposted to the right. (There is alternative parking here. Turning right, go through the gate and along the lateral track.

2. Short of the next track-gate, cross the wall-stile or go through the galvanised gate on the left to enter the sheep pen. Pass up through two gates and embark on the steady ascent beside a rising fence.

3. At the first brow of **Pikes Edge**, you can veer right to stand beside an impressive **currick** (or shepherds' lookout) perched on a boulder. *Other casually added cairns litter the continuing edge, all commanding a grand view down*

Dentdale. Ingleborough and Whernside are strong presences to the southwest and the roof of England forms the far north-western focus, centred on the Scafells. Keep with the rising fence to reach the moorland plateau and the **summit of Great Knoutberry Hill** where a stone-built **OS pillar** is located. A walker-friendly **wall-seat** lies over two adjacent stiles, providing an east/west wind-break.

4. Hold faith with the continuing wall drifting down south-eastward, crossing a **line of sink holes**. Step over the wall corner stile on to the open track. Turn right, following the **Pennine Bridleway** track to reach a four-way fingerpost.

5. Go through the adjacent gate, with the lateral **colliery track** from the Coal Road coming down by the sheep handling pen. Join the track signposted 'Stone House'. It descends **Arten Gill** via gates and passes under the **viaduct** carrying the **Settle-Carlisle Railway** to enter the hamlet of **Artengill**. The tidy order of the community gives little hint to its former industrial life, explained on the **interpretative panel**.

Men of stone: *Gritsone cairns on Pikes Edge looking towards Ingleborough*

6. Turn right along the valley road, crossing **Stonehouse Bridge** and following it in harmony with the **Dales Way**. The road hugs the banks of the **River Dee** as it flows down past **The Sportsman's Inn** to cross the next road bridge at **Cowgill**.

The Hollins at Cowgill is home to the Dent Brewery, a popular micro-brewery which began life in 1990.

7. After the bridge, heed the high-set road sign's guidance by heading right, winding up the bank for 1 kilometre to return to **Dent Station** and complete the walk. ♦

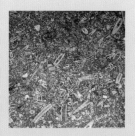

Dent 'black marble'
Fireplaces made from Dent black marble and featuring its characteristic white fossil patterns were being exported worldwide by the middle of the 19th century. The most celebrated was made in 1843 for the Russian Tsar's winter palace in St Petersburg. Sadly, the Stonehouse mill was forced out of business by cheap Italian marble, but a fine specimen of its craftsmanship can still be seen at Dent Heritage Centre.

Limestone pavement above Batty Green looking to Ingleborough and Ribblehead Viaduct

Whernside

A processional yet richly rewarding fell round — notable for the spellbinding fell-top view

What to expect:
Well-walked hill paths, some pitched; valley tracks

Distance/time: 13km/ 8 miles. Allow 5½ hours

Start/finish: Lay-by parking close to Ribblehead at the B6479/ B6255 junction

Grid ref: SD 764 792

Ordnance Survey Map: Explorer OL2 Yorkshire Dales: *Southern & Western areas: Whernside, Ingleborough & Pen-y-ghent*

After the walk: The Station Inn at Ribblehead and the Hill Inn at Chapel-le-Dale. Summer ice-cream van at the B6479/B6255 junction

Walk outline

This round trip is etched on to the fellside with considerable stretches of pitching and slabs, installed to cope with the inevitable and constant procession of appreciative disciples. The summit ridge is a grand promenade, reached by a suitably circuitous route, easing the gradient and throughout, the views sustain interest. The walk begins with the majesty of the Ribblehead Viaduct and ends through a pastoral limestone vale decked with quiet farmsteads.

Whernside

At 736 metres/2,415 feet this is the highest ground in the Yorkshire Dales National Park. In view is the neighbouring table-topped mesa of Ingleborough, dominating broad views to the south, while to the north the walker can see the sleek Howgill Fells beyond Dentdale.

The name Whernside derives from 'the summer pasture where mill-stones were got'. Once upon a time, the fell's high band of millstone grit was cut and chiselled into grind stones to be carried down for the multitude of pre-Industrial Revolution mills powering the rural economy.

Pitched path on Whernside

Northern brown argus

The Walk

1. Park on the verge beyond the cattle-grid or in the vicinity of the road junction east of the **Station Inn**. Follow the open track northwest — signposted 'Blea Moor Common'. Whernside, forming the high skyline ahead, is a powerful draw above the impressive **Ribblehead Viaduct**.

The 24-arched viaduct stretching for 400 metres across the moor is a serene and beautiful sight today and a staggering achievement of Victorian engineering. Irish rural depression brought thousands to labour in such colossal construction projects across Britain in the middle of the Victorian age. It took about 6,000 navvies a staggering five years to build the 70-mile Settle-Carlisle Railway. It opened first for freight in 1875, and then a year later for passengers.

As many as 2,000 navvies were based in this area alone, creating industrial bricks, excavating the Blea Moor Tunnel and raising the viaduct.

2. Some 150 metres short of the grand parade of 24 arches, a footpath forks at a signpost. Follow the path right, rising with pitched sections beside the **railway embankment**. It wends on adjacent to the track, later passing the **signal box** and former signalman's house.

3. Cross **Little Dale Beck** before veering over the **railway** via a bridge that carries two drove lanes either side of the **Force Gill aqueduct** — an

Fall on the fells: *A party of walkers pauses below the spectacular Force Gill waterfall*

unusual combination. *While down-track Ingleborough dominates, you can see the southern mouth of Blea Moor Tunnel up-track. Above are three shaft extraction spoil banks.*

4. As the path advances towards a hand-gate at the top of a short rise, you may veer left with minimal hint of path to inspect the noble **Force Gill waterfall** spilling over a broad ledge into a grand amphitheatre, aftre which the stream is named. Backtrack to continue. The trail is well secured with pitching on the next rise through the rushes, but becomes a rough path higher as it approaches a fence-stile.

5. Cross the stile as the path turns from northwest to west. It rises beside a wall that straddles a band of mountain limestone with tell-tale **sink holes** adjacent. The path strikes diagonally up the scarp bank to join the ridge wall on a southerly course to the **summit**, a handsome promenade. A squeeze-stile provides access to the OS column on **top of Whernside**.

Victorian wonder: *The valley-spanning, twenty-four arch Ribblehead Viaduct*

6. Thread back through the squeeze-stile and head south. The path descends via a kissing-gate, losing then regaining an accompanying wall over **High Pike**. The modern trail steps down and then veers off the ridge on a very steeply pitched descent. Slow progress is inevitable here, but, in its own way, absorbing. After a wall-gate, the trail traverses rough pasture — sometimes on slabs — going through two gates along the way. A lane is reached beside a **small stone barn**.

Interestingly, the adjacent wall is set on a limestone outcropping. You may like to visit the small **limekiln** about 20 metres to the right, where the 'Three Peaks Walk' route is signposted at the lane junction — a brief detour.

7. Turn left through the hand-gate by the stone barn — signposted 'Winterscales'. Traverse the pasture to pass in front of **Broadrake farmhouse**. Pass on by the barns, with waymarking guiding you through the field and the low limestone scar of **Broad Rake** close by on the left. Continue via a succession of gates, latterly on a track, to reach **Ivescar**. Pass straight on

between the farm buildings, keeping northeast, at first with the road signed to Winterscales. But, on passing a random collection of limestone boulders, keep right, along the open road leading to **Gunnerfleet**.

8. Cross the bridge spanning **Winterscales Beck**, advancing with the open track beneath the sturdy legs of the **Ribblehead viaduct**. Rejoin your outward route to complete the walk. ♦

Blea Moor Tunnel

While all eyes admire the gracious span of the Ribblehead Viaduct, spare a thought for the Herculean effort involved in the creation of Blea Moor Tunnel. At 2,876 metres long, it was largely dug by hand by navvies, with steam engines hauling the hard-won rock up shafts, evidenced in six huge heaps to this day. All manner of discomfort endured and no few deaths, the final brick-arching inserted in 1874.

Ingleborough with a huge glacial 'erratic' perched on limestone pavement

Ingleborough

An abundance of limestone features and an amazing gritstone plateau on the pick of the Yorkshire Three Peaks

What to expect:
Firm tracks; well-maintained fell paths

Distance/time: 15km/ 9½ miles. Allow 6 hours

Start/finish: National Park pay & display car park in Clapham

Grid ref: SD 745 692

Ordnance Survey Map: Explorer OL2 Yorkshire Dales: *Southern & Western areas: Whernside, Ingleborough & Pen-y-ghent*

After the walk: The New Inn Hotel and Croft Café beside the car park in Clapham

Walk outline

Ingleborough makes for one of the truly great fell days in the National Park. A wooded dale leads by the mouth of Ingleborough Cave through a romantic craggy defile onto the open moor. The walk takes leave of the sub-moor by a paved trail climbing to the high plateau. Coming onto the summit we orbit the scenic edges of this plateau. Escaping east, the walk ventures downhill via a wide expanse of untamable surface limestone. It then comes upon a winding green trail that ultimately reconnects with the Clapdale approach.

Ingleborough

This stand alone iconic mountain, rising to 723 metres/2,372 feet, is composed of layers of rock, beautifully revealed during this walk. From the bed of Silurian shales in Clapham, the walker comes quickly to the gleaming white carboniferous limestone rising above Clapdale to witness a moorland stream consumed by Gaping Gill. Climbing the mountain are dark bands of gritstone, originally formed in an ancient river delta. The daleside scars and semi-dissolved surface plates of limestone were scoured by ancient ice sheets.

Gaping Gill cavern

Common rock-rose

The Walk

1. Leave the **village car park**, bearing right and then left over the little packhorse-style bridge spanning **Clapdale Beck**. Wend your way up **Riverside**, passing the original editorial home of The Dalesman magazine.

Passing the **Church Avenue** junction next to **St James' Church**, continue by the **falls** to arrive at the entrance to **Clapdale** proper. Ingleborough Hall Estate offers public access for a fee to its private drive beside the lake.

2. Penniless walkers can side-step this Nature Trail by following the lane a bit further to a junction, embarking on the farm track on the right. This bridleway is signposted to 'Ingleborough Cave, Gaping Gill and Ingleborough'. The track has its own scenic merit, rising above the trees to view Thwaite Scars on the far side of Clapdale. Pass through the yard of **Clapdale Farm** and, from the gate at the end, descend naturally into the valley. At a fence-stile, you join forces with the estate drive to arrive at **Ingleborough Cave**.

3. The track goes through a gate and soon the dale constricts. After the next gate, the trail turns a corner and is confronted by the picturesque and impressive dry ravine of **Trow Gill**. You will find the tumble of rocks awkward as you thread through the tight exit at its top. Follow on with a

0   1km

1 mile

Limestone country: *A track snakes through limestone pavement below Ingleborough*

snaking wall in the dry valley and duly cross the twin ladder-stile.

4. The popular path leads on past two **potholes** to reach a fork in the way after 400 metres.

The right-hand track leads to the shocking, dark hole of **Gaping Gill**, where **Fell Beck** plunges underground into a deep cavern the size of a cathedral. *The utmost caution is required should you be tempted to step down to get up close and personal!*

The main route, however, goes left. This duly sets to work on sections of gravel and paving slabs to climb the steep southeast flank of **Little Ingleborough**. The paving forms steps higher up, passing a large, ragged cairn as the crest is neared.

5. Continue along the comparatively **narrow south ridge**. There is a rise and then one final, more concerted step up to an **interpretative panel**. The path angles up to draw you to the centre of the table-top.

A stroll orbiting the perimeter of the

Stormlight: *A low winter sun colours the trees below a silhouetted Ingleborough*

plateau, where there is evidence of ramparts, is a must, although most settle on the **summit cross-wall** for a wind-lee break. *The view northwest to Ribblehead, the famous viaduct, and beyond Whernside to the distant Howgills all give plenty of good reason to stay and enjoy your time after the effort of the long ascent.*

6. Exit the plateau via the narrow stony edge of **Swine's Tail** at the north-western corner of the summit. The popular trail swings down and across the long southern slopes of **Simon Fell Breast**, heading for a twin ladder-stile. Beyond this, walk beside a wall and past a roofless **shooting box** to cross a **ford** and pass through a hand-gate.

7. As the path forks, hold to the right-hand green way. There are old **stone grouse butts** nearby. Soon, **limestone pavement** grabs the attention as a green track weaves through a cut passage in the rocks. After crossing the line of a broken wall and shortly after the clints are lost, veer right again, now with the acorn waymarking of the **Pennine Bridleway** as your guide on **Long Scar**.

8. The green way drifts easily down,

passing close to a wall corner as it does so. Descend through the pastures and, after the second gate, go through a holding pen. This is followed by a track, but you need to watch for a ladder-stile that enables you to skip over the adjacent wall. Now descend the bank to a further ladder-stile and enter the dry valley directly below **Trow Gill**. From here, retrace your steps through **Clapdale** to complete the walk. ♦

The 'Dalesman'

Clapham was the birthplace of The Dalesman *magazine, which has reflected the life of the Dales since 1939. Founder Harry Scott was succeeded by Bill Mitchell MBE. Bill had a 40-year association, mostly as editor, and continues his prodigious output of Dales and Cumbrian books, presently numbering 160! A memorial to Harry, in the form of a wrought-iron gate, is located on the way to the Village Hall from Riverside.*

Pen-y-ghent rises above the autumn fells

Pen-y-ghent

Essentially a simple hill-walk, yet brimming with the geological essence of the National Park

What to expect:
Constructed fell paths; worn-earth fell paths; stone tracks

Distance/time: 9.5km/ 6 miles. Allow 4¼ hours

Start/finish: National Park pay & display car park in Horton-in-Ribblesdale

Grid ref: SD 807 725

Ordnance Survey Map: Explorer OL2 Yorkshire Dales: *Southern & Western areas: Whernside, Ingleborough & Pen-y-ghent*

After the walk: Pen-y-ghent Café, Blind Beck Tearooms, Golden Lion and Crown Hotel, all in Horton

Walk outline

Go climb your mountain and be chuffed you did. Of the beetling Three Peaks, this is the Ringo Starr, beating its own drum. An up-and-over climb, it incorporates lovely contact with limestone country features, particularly if a moment is given to carefully view the impressive Hull Pot. The walk ends with a scenic stroll down Horton Scar Lane. It's an expedition of the well trammelled kind, but fabulously worthy for all that.

Pen-y-ghent

Pen-y-ghent is a very commanding presence in upper Ribblesdale. The distinctive cap of millstone grit rests on a sequence of Carboniferous limestone beds, the whole resisting the weathering onslaught of ice to give an eye-catching must-climb headland above the village of Horton-in-Ribblesdale. The under-moor of 'hollow' limestone is riddled with caverns where streams are lost to sunlight, invariably emerging as gushing watercourses where they encounter the impervious Silurian shales in the valley floor of Ribblesdale.

Hull pot

Purple saxifrage

The Walk

1. Turn right out of the car park and follow the footway beside the **B6479**, passing the **Pen-y-ghent café** (Tourist Information Centre). After the **church**, cross the road bridge spanning **Douk Ghyll** and bear left along the side road.

2. The road rises to **Brackenbottom Farm**. At the first barn, heed the signpost 'Pen-y-ghent summit' directing you left via hand-gates. Embark on a steady pasture climb with a drystone wall on the left. Two modest limestone rock-steps lead to a wall-stile; otherwise, it's hand-gates and pitching to the ridge-top to join the **Pennine Way**.

3. Turn up left on a stone-pitched trail towards the southern 'nose' of Pen-y-ghent. The path naturally veers right as the upper tier of limestone looms. This rock hazard is taken by small, natural steps. The path winds upwards to the topmost gritstone tier where a genuine rock-step demands steady handling. The path eases onto the **summit of Pen-y-ghent**

where you find a small **cairn and OS column** at 694 metres/2,277 feet.

4. Cross the adjacent wall-stile and walk away from the wall on a trail which drifts easily down the fellside, veering from northwest to north along the edge. The path drops to a footpath sign with a limestone cliff ahead.

The crag is a precious habitat of the rare and delicate Alpine purple saxifrage.

5. The gravel path leads down to a gate/ladder-stile. After some 400 metres, watch for a pasture path veering back left. This is a spur route, allowing you to cautiously inspect **Hunt Pot**, a deep pothole consuming the watercourse draining the fell's western slopes. Regain the trail and, after a double ladder-stile/

Ever upward: *The wallside path from Brackenbottom look towards Pen-y-ghent*

gate, you reach a gate giving access to **Horton Scar Lane**.

6. Before setting off down the lane, you are encouraged to make a there-and-back visit to inspect **Hull Pot** — by following the track right for 400 metres.

A tiny beck enters the limestone under-world at Hull Pot, spilling 20 metres into a great hollow, a collapsed cavern.

From Hull Pot, backtrack and follow Horton Scar Lane south, all the way to the **village** street. Go right to return to the car park and complete the walk. ♦

'Yorkshire Three Peaks' challenge

Horton-in-Ribblesdale has become synonymous with the Yorkshire Three Peaks Walk, taking in the summits of Pen-y-ghent, Whernside and Ingleborough at the head of Ribblesdale. While many see it as a race, others see sufficient challenge just in completing the 38km/ 23 mile walk. The Yorkshire Dales National Park runs a voluntary 'Friends of the Three Peaks' project, the proceeds of which go towards the upkeep of paths along the route.

Useful Information

'Welcome to Yorkshire'
This comprehensive website draws together a wealth of information about visiting Yorkshire. **www.yorkshire.com**

Yorkshire Dales National Park
For in-depth information about the National Park, including 'What's on' listings of local events and tourist information. **www.yorkshiredales.org.uk**

Visitor Centres
Many towns in the area have Tourist Information Centres where staff will help with accommodation, heritage and outdoor activities. The main ones are listed here; there are also National Park Centres in some key locations.

Tourist Information Centres

Horton-in-Ribblesdale	01729 860333	horton@ytbtic.co.uk
Ingleton	01524 241049	ingleton@ytbtic.co.uk
Leyburn	01748 828747	ticleyburn@richmondshire.co.uk
Sedbergh	01539 620125	tic@sedbergh.org.uk
Settle	01729 825192	settle@ytbtic.co.uk
Skipton	01756 792809	skipton@ytbtic.co.uk

National Park Centres
Open daily April-October; limited in winter; closed in January

Aysgarth Falls	01969 662910	aysgarth@yorkshiredales.org.uk
Grassington	01756 751690	grassington@yorkshiredales.org.uk
Hawes	01969 666210	hawes@yorkshiredales.org.uk
Malham	01969 652380	malham@yorkshiredales.org.uk
Reeth	01748 884059	reeth@yorkshiredales.org.uk

Emergencies
If you have an accident whilst out walking and are immobilised, call 112 on your mobile 'phone, ask for the police, and tell them to contact mountain rescue. Be ready to tell the operator your exact location (nearest village, plus features named on the map close to your location) and the nature of your injury.

Weather
For the latest report for the Yorkshire Dales follow the link on the National Park website (see above) for 'Weather'. For details of local weather, go to **www.mylocalweather.org.uk** and click on the area you're interested in.